Love Charms

Love Charms

Spells, potions, tokens, and incantations

by Jennifer Knapp

illustrations by Annika Smajic

CHRONICLE BOOKS

SAN FRANCISCO

✳ ○ ✳

Library of Congress Cataloging-in-Publication Data:
Knapp, Jennifer.
Love charms : spells, potions, tokens, and incantations / by Jennifer
Knapp ; illustrations by Annika Smajic.
p. cm.
ISBN 0-8118-3968-0
1. Magic. 2. Love–Miscellanea. 3. Charms. 4. Magic, Celtic.
I. Title.
BF1623.L6 K53 2003
133.4'42—dc21
2002014143

Manufactured in China.

Designed by Vanessa Dina

Distributed in Canada by Raincoast Books
9050 Shaughnessy Street
Vancouver, British Columbia V6P 6E5

10 9 8 7 6 5 4 3 2 1

Chronicle Books LLC
85 Second Street
San Francisco, California 94105

www.chroniclebooks.com

For my honey.

✴ ◦ ✳

Double, double, toil and trouble . . .
Unbounded thanks to the jinxiest of covens:
the High Priestess Mikyla Bruder, the Goddess Leslie Jonath,
Annika Smajic, Leslie Davisson, Jodi Davis,
Vanessa Dina, and Tera Killip.

Introduction

He loves me; he loves me not . . .

The yeses and noes of the daisy's petals have been raising hopes and breaking hearts for centuries, proof that the mystery of love endures. Today, this simple tradition may be nothing more than a school yard pastime, and yet such rituals have come down to us through the ages, with generations of amorous lovers having vouched for their usefulness (petal plucking is actually an old Anglo-Saxon love divination charm). All the scientific advances in the world haven't solved the enigma of love, and so the question remains: Can centuries of love charms be wrong?

Lucky for us, early matchmakers put brush to papyrus and recorded their findings for future lonely hearts. In fact, written love charms are among the earliest known documents, dating between 2400 and 1900 B.C., and hailing from Egypt, Persia, and China. Magical words and images were inscribed on clay talismans, engraved on gem amulets, and later cast in metal jewelry. These ancient Indo-European tribal practices went on to form the basis of Celtic magic, a rich tradition whose heyday lasted from 700 B.C. to A.D. 100.

A Celtic priestess filled her days with healing, midwifery, blessings, cursings, and even dealing with the unruly weather. But one of her most important jobs was hooking people up. Using common herbs, incantations, and a few exotic ingredients, she put together a spell, potion, or talisman to straighten out a wayward wife, tame a bothersome boyfriend, or plant the seed of romance in an unsuspecting crush.

The nature-based belief system of the Celts came to be called paganism by the Romans (the Latin *paganus* means "country dweller"). Christians vilified its practitioners as witches, claiming they cavorted with the devil. Burnings, hangings, and drownings ensued. Despite the persecution, love charms lived on. Charms, spells, and incantations went underground, cleverly disguised as enticing perfumes, delectable potions, and folkloric rhymes. Practiced behind closed doors, love magic eventually became a tradition marginalized by the mainstream—an old wives' tale, a frivolous pastime.

Today, love remains as perplexing as ever. Even with e-mails, faxes, and cell phones, the age-old question lingers: Will he call me, or will he call me not? Rather than wondering, take charge of your love life. If you can't persuade your broomstick to sweep, let alone fly, don't fret.

The recipes and ideas in these pages are adapted from centuries of know-how with a healthy pinch of modernity stirred in, so you won't need to slave all day over a hot cauldron or behead any cute little froggies. They require only the most enchanting of ingredients, and the resulting potions, spells, and tokens of affection are as sweet as a first kiss.

Begin at the beginning, chapter 1, "Bewitch—Finding True Love," and check out your future honeys with the help of a fragrant Celtic dream sachet and a mesmerizing minty love potion. When you've found Mr. Right, move onto chapter 2, "Bedazzle—Drawing Love In," and see what you pull out of the hat. The oh-so-sweetheart candy spell is just one of many charms with the perfect ingredients for romance. Once your path crosses with "the One," don't let your bright and shiny new love get away. Stoke the fire under the cauldron and flip directly to the love spells in chapter 3, "Beguile—Head-over-Heels in Love." And if a black cat crosses your path, don't panic. Just turn to chapter 4, "Bedevil—Easing the Heartache." You'll find all you need to get love back on track.

Ready to bewitch, bedazzle, and beguile? Let's begin.

Chapter 1:

Bewitch–Finding True Love

You're scooting along merrily on your broomstick with your hair in a ponytail when, yikes! Mr. Valentine's Day pops his big red head over the horizon. Now all you need is a sweetheart to wipe that smirk off his face. Easier said than done? In a pinch, try this modern charm: Fill the fridge with beer, order a pizza, and yell incantations at attractive passersby. If that fails, maybe the pizza delivery guy will be cute. Better yet, keep your pointy hat on straight and, instead of hooking up with a rat—however cute and whiskery he may be—set the scene for head-over-heels romance with the love-drawing charms in this chapter.

Even if you live in a studio apartment—rather than a more appropriate Gothic castle—you can still conjure up plenty of hocus-pocus. First, you'll need a place to park your cauldron. Clear a small table of your mumble jumble to make room for your mumbo jumbo. Place the table in front of a window so that your potions will be exposed to the enlightening sun and mysterious moon. Keep the table clear–find a new home for your trashy magazines and random hair clips—and use it only for creating charms.

Creating Your Altar

Pink silk scarf

6 small bottles and vials for holding potions and philters

Love-Drawing Altar Candle (page 16)

Incense coal and saucer

Come Hither, Now! Incense (page 18)

Box of matches

Small mixing bowl

Love-attracting items such as rosemary, lavender, copal, cinnamon, lemon, rose quartz, rose petals, daisies, and pennies

In preparation for creating your first love charms, cleanse the table of any mundane residue from its old life as an abandoned-junk repository. Spread the pink scarf over the top (pink radiates romance). Collect the materials listed (left) and arrange on the table. Burn a chip of copal resin on the incense coal. Now your altar is ready. Let the bewitching begin!

Bewitching Basics

○ ○ ○ ○

YOUR ALTAR MUST POSSESS THE ENERGY OF THE FOUR
ELEMENTS: A CANDLE REPRESENTS FIRE; INCENSE SMOKE
REPRESENTS AIR; A BOWL OF SPRINGWATER OR A SEASHELL
REPRESENTS WATER; AND HERBS, FLOWERS, AND STONES
REPRESENT THE EARTH.

Candles add the element of fire to your charms,
an essential ingredient for romance, love, and passion.
Boost this fiery mojo by decorating your votive
holders with love deity images. There's nothing like a
few thousand-year-old goddesses to lend a hand.
They've seen it all.

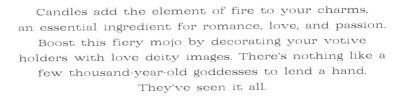

Love-Drawing Altar Candle

Glue

Red, pink, and clear glitter

Color copies of your favorite love deity (Venus is always a good choice), reduced or enlarged as necessary to about 4 by 8 inches

Red, pink, and clear tiny plastic jewels

Votive candles in tall glass holders

Scissors

Clear tape

Using glue and lots of glitter, dress up your paper deity. Glue on tiny plastic jewels. Despite their above-it-all demeanor, deities love to look glamorous. Let dry.

Wrap a paper diety around the glass exterior of each candle, trimming with scissors to fit as necessary, and tape in place. It helps if, while you're snipping and gluing, you ask your chosen deity, very politely, for her assistance with your project. Make a few candles, using a variety of goddesses, to make sure you have all your bases covered.

∽ Love Lore ∾

VENUS-VA-VOOM—VENUS, KNOWN AS
APHRODITE TO THE GREEKS, IS *THE*
GODDESS OF LOVE. AND NO ONE PLAYS
THE DATING GAME BETTER. BORN IN
THE OCEAN, SHE IS KNOWN TO LOUNGE
IN A CLAMSHELL IN HER OFF-HOURS.
BUT WHEN THE PINK LOVE-PHONE
RINGS, SHE LEAPS INTO HER VENUS-
MOBILE AND SPEEDS OFF TO FIGHT THE
WORST COMMITMENT-PHOBE. SURE
SHE'S HAD HER FAIR SHARE OF DAY-
TIME DRAMA IN THE ROMANCE
DEPARTMENT, BUT SHE ALWAYS COMES
THROUGH WITH GRACE. USE HER
IMAGE ON YOUR CHARMS AND HER
NAME IN YOUR INCANTATIONS.

Come Hither, Now! Incense

In Mexico, *botanicas* are stocked with powdered
incenses for improving every aspect of life,
from drawing wealth to repelling evil. This particular
incense is guaranteed to open your life to love.
Burn it while you're creating charms to imbue
them with love-drawing power. Lovely, pungent
lavender attracts romantic love, and feisty lemongrass
draws pure love. Mastic was used by the ancient
Romans in love magic, and they chewed it to
sweeten their kisses, too!

Using the back of a spoon, crush together
1 tablespoon each dried lavender, lemongrass, and
mastic. Stir in 1 tablespoon cornstarch. Add
extra zing to the charm with a few drops of lavender
or lemon oil. Sprinkle 1 teaspoon of the mixture
on the center of a lighted incense coal.

Bewitching Basics

○ ○ ○ ○

THINK ABOUT GROWING YOUR OWN HERBS IN A SUNNY
KITCHEN WINDOW. THAT WAY YOU CAN START POURING YOUR
LOVE INTO THEM FROM THE FIRST SIGN OF A SPROUT, AND THEY
WON'T COME INTO CONTACT WITH ANY BAD INFLUENCES. IT'S
BEEN PROVEN THAT PLANTS LIKE TO BE TALKED TO, NOT TO
MENTION THEIR INTEREST IN STYLISH MACRAMÉ GARB. TREAT
YOUR PLANTS WELL, AND THEY WILL TREAT YOU WELL, EVEN IF
YOU EAT THEM! LAVENDER, ROSEMARY, LEMON VERBENA,
MARJORAM, AND MINT WILL GET YOU ON YOUR WAY TO LOVE,
AND YOU MIGHT EVEN WOW THAT ATTRACTIVE STRANGER
WITH YOUR SPICY MASALA, TOO.

Be Mine Anointing Oils

Philters, small vials of oil imbued with magical proper-
ties, were popular in medieval love magic. The word
philter comes from the ancient Greek word *philtron*,
meaning "to love." Use these oil combinations to anoint
your candles, charms, and even yourself.

In one of your vials, create a philter for drawing love.
Mix a few drops of Celtic rosemary and lavender oils
to attract true love. Or combine drops of ancient
Persian jasmine, rose, and clove oils for passionate love.

Anoint an altar candle by dropping a few beads of
rosemary or lavender oil onto your finger, and then
swirling it clockwise around the unlighted candle from
the base to the top and finally along the wick. Dab a
drop behind your ears while you're at it.

Bewitching Basics

○ ○ ○ ○

WHEN BREWING UP TROUBLE, IT'S IMPERATIVE THAT YOU
USE ONLY THE BEST INGREDIENTS. THE FINEST ORGANIC HERBS
AND FLOWERS AND PURE ESSENTIAL OILS ARE THE WAY TO GO.
THEY MAY COST A BIT MORE, BUT THEY WILL ENSURE
ENCHANTING RESULTS EVERY TIME. MANY OF THE HISTORICALLY
IMPORTANT INGREDIENTS FOR WHICH TITANIA WOULD HAVE
HOCKED HER TIARA ARE NOW READILY AVAILABLE AT YOUR
LOCAL HEALTH FOOD STORE. DRIED HERBS, FLOWERS,
AND ESSENTIAL OILS SHOULD HAVE A FRESH, COLORFUL
APPEARANCE (NOT BAT-WING BROWN) AND SHOULD SMELL
PUNGENT (NOT LIKE A COBWEBBY ATTIC). FOR MORE ON
FINDING HERBS AND OILS, SEE PAGES 130-131.

Create a jewel-encrusted box to hold your wishes for a sweetie. Try out your Come Hither, Now! Incense during a simple spell that asks the starlight, star bright to twinkle down and make all your wishes come true.

Wish upon a Star Spell

Glue

Small empty, square tissue box

5 color copies of a love deity

Craft knife

Red, pink, and clear glitter

Plastic jewels

Pink votive candle

Matches

Come Hither, Now! Incense (page 18)

Fresh pink rose petals

Rose quartz stone

Scissors

Sheet of pink writing paper

Pen with red ink

Using glue, decorate the box on all sides including the top with the images of the love deity. Using the craft knife, trim off any excess paper and make a new opening in the top of the box. Embellish by gluing on the glitter and plastic jewels. Let dry.

Set the box in the center of the altar table on a clear night during the waxing moon. Light the candle and the incense and place them next to your box. Open the window and find a star that attracts your attention. Holding the rose petals and rose quartz in one hand, visualize the starlight beaming down and charging the petals and stone with its twinkliness. Carefully place the petals and stone through the hole of the decorated box.

continued

22

Using the scissors, cut the sheet of paper into small strips. Relax completely and empty your mind of that huge Rolodex of things that need doing. Using the pen, write a trait you are looking for in a honey on each slip of paper. Maybe you desire a brainiac with the flashy moves of Bruce Lee, the faithfulness of Myron (your dog), and the honesty of Abe Lincoln. Hold on, Ms. Frankenstein! If you want to get things rolling in the hay right away, you should instead concentrate on the basic necessities, such as not leaving dirty dishes in the sink and putting the seat down on the toilet. Okay, maybe faithfulness and honesty are less far-fetched! One by one, place each strip into the wish box.

Keep the box near the window to be charged nightly by the stars. By the next waxing moon, he will come knocking.

∾ Love Lore ∾

OSHÙN, THE YORUBAN GODDESS OF LOVE, TURNS UP IN SANTERIA, A SYNCRETISTIC CARRIBBEAN RELIGION THAT BLENDS YORUBAN TRADITIONS WITH ROMAN CATHOLIC SAINTS. WHEN ASKING OSHÙN TO HELP YOU WITH YOUR CHARMS, GAIN HER FAVOR WITH HONEY AND THE OCCASIONAL CIGAR.

Heavenly Hair

✴ ✴ ✴

Luscious lemons are native to India and have
been used in Eastern love and beauty rituals for
millennia. Celtic women rinsed their lovely locks in
lemon juice mixed with lavender flowers to draw love.
This particular formula will make your hair shiny
and sweet smelling, perfect for swinging around
and releasing its lemony magic.

Squeeze the juice of 1 lemon into a bowl. Strain
the juice through cheesecloth to remove all the seeds
and pulp. Add 6 drops lavender oil. After shampooing,
conditioning, and rinsing your hair, pour the lemon
mixture through it. Massage the mixture into your
hair and rinse with water. If you're in a hurry, simply
add lemon and lavender oils to your conditioner.

Lucky Seven Love-Drawing Pouches

✷ ✷ ✷

Find the falling-at-your-feet adoration you deserve.
Try the first three charms for general love drawing
and the last four for various romantic adventures.

To invoke the power of the charms, light the Love-
Drawing Altar Candle (page 16) and Come Hither, Now!
Incense (page 18). Sprinkle a 7-inch circle of rosemary,
lavender, or glitter on the altar table. Cut out a
6-inch square of red silk or velvet and place it
inside the circle. Choose one of the following charm
mixtures and place its ingredients on the center of
the cloth, all the while visualizing your objective.
Trap your romantic notions inside the square by
gathering up the corners and tying them together
with a red or pink silk ribbon. Draw your finger across
the circle to break the line and release the wooing
magic. Wear the pouch at all times, on your right side
for a faithful love, on your left for a passionate love,
and around your neck for a balance of the two.

Love-Drawing Pouch

No. 1: for a fun fling

You may not want to tie yourself down with weighty romance, but who isn't up for some fun? These traditional Celtic love-drawing ingredients are spiced up with some potent pepper and sassy salt. The cheeky cherry arouses amorous thoughts.

3 fresh pink rose petals

1 tablespoon fresh rosemary

Splash of springwater

Chip of rose quartz

Pinch of salt

Dash of dried and ground cayenne pepper

1 dried cherry

Complete your love-drawing pouch by following the directions on facing page.

Love-Drawing Pouch

No. 2: For the Real Thing Romance

Red wine is often used in love charms as a substitute for blood—good news for the squeamish! Roses, rose quartz, and lavender have long been used to draw love, most notably in medieval times. An acorn attracts strength and faithfulness. Honey balances the mix with a drop of sweet romance.

7 fresh red rose petals

1 teaspoon fresh or dried lavender

Chip of rose quartz

1 acorn

3 drops red wine

A few drops rainwater

$1/4$ teaspoon vanilla oil or extract

$1/4$ teaspoon honey

Complete your love-drawing pouch by following the directions on page 26.

Love-Drawing Pouch

No. 3: for Pure Passion

Enough of the hug and cuddle! Here's
the down and dirty. Orange blossoms
draw and bind romantic love. Cinnamon
and clove, appreciated for their ability
to spark lust in the Middle East and
China, heat things up. Tabasco, used
in Louisiana voodoo circles, gives this
spell its whoo! While stripy tigereye
adds a passionate grrrr!

**1 fresh orange blossom or a bit
of orange peel**

1 teaspoon ground cinnamon

A few whole cloves

Dash of Tabasco sauce

Fresh tiger lily petal

Chip of tigereye

1 drop jasmine oil

Complete your love-drawing pouch by
following the directions on page 26.

Love-Drawing Pouch

No. 4: for Getting the Sweet Stuff

Everything a girl adores. It's no
coincidence that chocolate appears on
Valentine's Day in big red boxes. Its
ability to seduce has been known for
hundreds of years and is just now being
analyzed by the big brains. But who
cares why it works! Have a nibble while
making this charm and savor that
luscious, melting, weak-at-the-knees
feeling. A sunny daisy boosts your
flirting abilities.

1 chocolate kiss

Pinch of pink glitter

1 fresh daisy

1 dried cherry

Pinch of sugar

3 drops jasmine oil

Complete your love-drawing pouch by
following the directions on page 26.

Love-Drawing Pouch

No. 5: for a Tropical Tryst

During the dismal, icy days of winter,
your dreams inevitably drift off on
coconut and banana breezes and wash up
on the sandy shores of some piña colada
island where a certain someone awaits
you. This especially intoxicating potion
makes the most of South Seas magic.
Ylang-ylang is used in bridal beds to
encourage lust, as it opens the mind,
frees the spirit, and inspires feelings of
joy. Seashells induce dreams of love, and
vanilla oil is an ancient aphrodisiac.

> 1 seashell
>
> Pinch of clear glitter
>
> 3 drops each coconut oil,
> vanilla oil, and ylang-ylang oil
>
> Splash of saltwater
>
> 1 fresh passionflower
>
> Green ribbon (rather than red
> or pink) for tying

Complete your love-drawing pouch by
following the directions on page 26.

Love-Drawing Pouch

No. 6: For a Sultry Arabian Night

Start practicing your belly wiggles.
Cinnamon and clove make any night as
hot as a harem tent in the desert.
Cardamom and ginseng spark lusty love.
Coriander has long been used in love
potions, encouraging serenity and peace.
Bells are used in Persian, Gypsy, and
Chinese love rituals. Marigolds not only
promote dreams of love, but will also
boost your energy for the dance of the
seven veils.

Pinch of ground cinnamon

3 whole cloves

1 cardamom pod

Pinch of dried ginseng

Chip of amber

3 drops coriander oil

Small bell

1 fresh marigold

Complete your love-drawing pouch by
following the directions on page 26.

No. 7: For a Weekend Romance in Paris

Do you dream of strolling in the Tuileries, holding hands under a café umbrella on the Boulevard Saint-Michel, and kissing at the top of the Eiffel Tower? This pouch will fly you there. Violets inspire love and promote peace. Champagne has been associated with amour since the first bubble tickled a nose in 1695. Top things off by wearing frilly undies, too, of course. *Très bien!*

3 drops champagne

1 chocolate kiss

1 drop of your favorite perfume

Pinch of silver or blue glitter

3 drops rainwater

1 fresh violet

Blue ribbon (rather than red or pink) for tying

Complete your love-drawing pouch by following the directions on page 26.

Stones are the oldest things on Earth. A beaded necklace is not only pretty, but the beads' ancient energy will help pull love in your direction and get your chakras doing the samba. Most bead shops stock polished stone beads in a variety of shapes and sizes.

Make sure the ones you choose have holes large enough for the ribbon to pass through. You will need one of each of the following stones below.

Shake Your Chakra Necklace

✫ ✫ ✫

Rose quartz for drawing love

Carnelian for drawing opportunities

Citrine for drawing friendship

Garnet for success in your spells of passion

Moonstone for feminine power

Lodestone for attracting love

Boji (use 2 stones together) for drawing and binding your love

Organza ribbon, 14 to 16 inches long and 1/4 inch wide, in a color of choice

String the 8 semiprecious stone beads, in any order, onto the ribbon. Space the stones about 1 inch apart. The width of the ribbon will hold the stones in place. Tie the ribbon around your neck with 3 knots.

Are you the type who has a long list of
turn-ons and -offs that you total up every time a
boy makes the mistake of saying hi? He has weird
pants, okay. But the Bee Gees hairdo? *Out!* If this
describes you, these two ultradiscerning charm
pouches are indispensable.

Miss Choosy Charms

✶ ✶ ✶

**Love-Drawing Altar candle
(page 16)**

**Come Hither, Now! Incense
(page 18)**

**6-inch square pink velvet,
cut into a heart shape**

3 fresh pink rose petals

1 fresh daisy

1/2 teaspoon dried lavender

1 drop jasmine oil

Dash of ground cinnamon

3 fresh or dried mint leaves

**1 small stone shaped
like a heart**

1 fresh honeysuckle blossom

1 penny

Blue ribbon tied in 7 knots

Prince Charming

If you're a pouting princess hanging out
down at the frog pond getting your lips all
slimy, then try this charm.

On the night of the new moon, light the
candle and burn the incense. In the center
of the heart, place the remaining ingredients, except the ribbon. Gather up the
edges and secure the ribbon. Place the
pouch on your heart and repeat:

*Oh Prince of mine
You are divine.*

*Give me your charms
And I'll fall in your arms.*

continued

6-inch square red silk

3 fresh red rose petals

1/2 teaspoon fresh
or dried rosemary

1/2 teaspoon
ground cinnamon

Chip of rose quartz

Knot of red ribbon

1 penny

Green ribbon
tied in 3 knots

Mr. Right

If a prince in a feathery lilac cap and ruffly blouse wouldn't fit in at your corner coffeehouse, it's time to move! But until the lease is up, bide your time with Mr. Right. Why does he always wear those khaki pants? That's a question you can ask when he comes knocking.

On a night of the waxing moon, cut out the red silk. Place the remaining ingredients, except the ribbon, in the center. Gather up the corners and secure with the green ribbon. Place the pouch on your heart, focus your mind, and repeat this charm:

**Mr. Right and
beautiful me
Together we are
meant to be.**

Bewitching Basics

○ ○ ○ ○

OVER THE MOON—LOVE CHARMS GENERALLY DRAW ON THE
ENTHRALLING LIGHT OF BOTH THE FULL AND WAXING MOON.
THE MOON HAS FOUR PHASES: THE FULL MOON, WHEN IT IS BIG,
ROUND, AND HAPPY; THE WANING MOON, WHEN IT IS SLOWLY
FADING TO DARKNESS; THE NEW MOON, WHEN IT IS A
THIN SLIVER; AND THE WAXING MOON, WHEN IT IS GRADUALLY
MOVING BACK TO FULLNESS.

Exotic scents, each whiff packed with powerful magic, have been enticing noses for centuries. Choose from mysterious Persian or East Indian mixtures, a fresh and pure Celtic blend, or a free-love free-for-all! Make extra batches because all your friends will want some, too! Beware to all those within sniffing distance!

Heaven Scent Solid Perfume

1/2 teaspoon beeswax

Small microwave-safe bowl

Wooden spoon

2 tablespoons almond oil

One of the following essential oil combinations:

Ancient Persian love scent of jasmine, rose, and sandalwood

Kama Sutra passion mixture of vanilla, sandalwood, jasmine, and vetiver

Love-inducing Celtic combo of rosemary, lavender, and lemon

Happy hippie love fest of patchouli, lavender, orange, lemongrass, and pine

Place the beeswax in the bowl and microwave on high until the beeswax has melted, about 1 minute. Do not overheat. Using the wooden spoon, stir the almond oil into the beeswax. Add 20 drops total of your essential oil combination of choice. Pour the perfume into an empty makeup or lip balm container and let cool.

If you prefer to use the classic cauldron method, heat the beeswax on the stove top in a double boiler. Remove from the heat and proceed as directed.

Bewitching Basics

○ ○ ○ ○

HEATING UP YOUR CONCOCTIONS IN AN IRON CAULDRON
IS NOT A GOOD IDEA, AS THE METAL CAN REACT WITH THE
HERBS AND ZAP THEIR STRENGTH. BUBBLE ALL POTIONS IN
A HEATPROOF GLASS OR ENAMEL-LINED POT, AND STIR IN A
CLOCKWISE DIRECTION TO INVOKE THE MAGIC. FOR THE
GIRL-ON-THE-GO, A MICROWAVE CAN SPEED UP THE CHARM-
MAKING PROCESS. USE A MICROWAVE-SAFE GLASS BOWL AND
BE CAREFUL NOT TO OVERHEAT THE OILS AND HERBS. STORE ALL
INGREDIENTS IN AIRTIGHT, DARK-COLORED GLASS CONTAINERS.

Titillating Tea Bath-Bags

When attracting that mystery date, it doesn't hurt
to smell divine! Make a relaxing soak for yourself using
these love-drawing herbs. Share your blissful smile
by making one for a friend, too!

Cut out an 8-inch square of cheesecloth. Choose one
of the following herbal baths and place the ingredients
in the center of the square. Add extra essential oils
as desired to make your nose do somersaults of joy.
Gather up the corners of the cheesecloth and tie
with a red or pink ribbon. Use an orange ribbon if
you're giving it to a friend. For a quick and easy
alternative, look for drawstring cheesecloth pouches
in kitchen shops.

Draw a hot bath, add the tea bath-bag, and enjoy
a long soak while thinking lovely thoughts.
Mmmm!

Tea Bath-Bag

No. 1: Giggle Bath

You'll want to luxuriate in this pungent
bath until you turn all pruney. And
what a lovely prune you'll be! Basil,
lavender, and rosemary inspire love in all
those who cross your path. Even the
gods are known to lose their heads for
lavender on a midsummer's eve.
Rosemary cleanses the body and mind,
delivering a physical and mental boost.

1 tablespoon dried basil

1 tablespoon dried rosemary

2 tablespoons dried lavender

6 drops lemon oil

Complete your tea-bag bath by
following the directions on page 40.

Tea Bath-Bag

No. 2: Groove Bath

Marjoram and rue attract love and provide protection from a broken heart. Rue also helps to purify and clear a cluttered mind, opening your heart to love. Jasmine, one of the oldest seducers, warms the heart and is used in Eastern magic as an aphrodisiac.

- 1/4 cup fresh or dried rose petals
- 1 tablespoon dried marjoram
- 1 tablespoon dried rue
- 6 drops jasmine oil

Complete your tea-bag bath by following the directions on page 40.

Tea Bath-Bag

No. 3: Glam Bath

Vervain attracts love and brings general good luck and wealth along with romance. Bathing in yarrow will help you find your mate in this incarnation or the next.

1 tablespoon dried yarrow
2 tablespoons dried rosemary
1 tablespoon dried vervain
6 drops lavender oil

Complete your tea-bag bath by following the directions on page 40.

Love Chi

✳ ✳ ✳

In China, *feng-shui* takes care of lonely heart pangs. Get your *chi* flowing by balancing your boudoir and opening the space to love. Create a "love" table to draw the perfect mate. Set a small table on the side of the bed where the dog sleeps. Place items on it that will draw a snuggly (and hopefully less hairy) bedmate. Choose tokens that represent the characteristics you desire in a mate. Girlie magazines and a remote control? Probably not. Remember, you're in charge here, so fill the table with things your dream match would possess. Maybe he reads Jane Austen novels, decorates with skateboard stickers, and eats red licorice. A soul mate! Once he arrives, don't let him screw up the *chi* with a pile of dirty socks on the floor.

 Herbs & Flowers

RED LICORICE IS OH-SO-YUMMY, BUT BLACK LICORICE IS THE REAL DEAL. FLAVORED WITH LICORICE ROOT AND SOMETIMES ANISEED, IT SPURS LUST, INSPIRES FIDELITY, AND IS USED IN THE LOVE SPELLS OF MANY CULTURES.

Where Is He Already? Divination

✳ ✳ ✳

When you find yourself tapping your toe and glancing repeatedly at your watch wondering how your spells are working, take a sneak peek. Charms and divination have gone hand in hand throughout history because, let's face it, we're an impatient bunch. Depending on how your spells are progressing, you'll know whether to dive into the deep end or run screaming in the opposite direction. The following are a few handy methods for divining the future.

Sweetheart Dreams Spell

Meadowsweet encourages love, balance, and harmony in your life, while hops guarantees a deep and visionary sleep. Peppermint has been used in Chinese herbology to induce sexual dreams and by the Hebrews as an aphrodisiac.

Fill a blue sachet pouch—blue brings on the kind of dreams that make you want to stay in bed all day—with 1 tablespoon dried lavender, $1/2$ tablespoon dried hops, and 1 tablespoon dried meadowsweet. Place the sachet under your pillow, then sip a small teacup full of mint tea flavored with a few drops of vanilla extract before falling asleep. You will dream of your future love.

Dreamy!

To inspire dreams of your love-to-be, try a few of these old European magical methods. Sleep with a mirror or a daisy under your pillow, wear your nightie inside out, or count 9 stars on 9 consecutive nights, and on the last night you will dream of your future mate.

On the night of the full moon, tie together a little bundle of fresh rosemary and thyme, and slip it into one of your shoes placed at the foot of your bed. Then gaze at the moon and repeat this old English rhyme:

> *Moon, moon, tell unto me*
> *When my true love I shall see*
> *What fine clothes am I to wear?*
> *How many children shall I bear?*
> *For if my love comes not to me*
> *Dark and dismal my life will be.*

Boo hoo! See if you can update this dark and dismal rhyme with some fempower, aided by tips from Incantation Writing 101 (page 67).

Party Trick! Palm Reading

Be the life of the party with or without a lampshade. Just make sure each guest crosses your palm with silver first. Begin by practicing on yourself. Turn your writing hand palm up. Gently pull the pinky finger slightly out to the side and away from the other fingers. A few small lines will form on the outer edge of your hand just below the place where the pinky meets the palm, and just above the lines that extend across the palm. Count these lines. The total represents the number of great romances you can expect in your life.

Chapter 2

Bedazzle—Drawing Love In

After successfully completing the
last chapter, you will have more
than enough messages on your
answering machine. But even
though you've drawn "the One" (and
probably a lot of innocent
bystanders) into your realm, you
can't be sure your catch has
figured out what's going on. Of
course, the first thing to do is walk
right up and spell it out. Then add
a few love-inspiring charms from
this chapter, and you'll be paving
the way for never-thought-it-could-
happen-to-me romance.

Spread a lavender silk scarf (lavender nurtures love) on your altar
table and gather a few of these
items to encourage love: clove,
camellia, comfrey, ginger, marjoram,
mimosa, meadowsweet, mint, violets, pansies, pomegranates, and rue.

It's You Baby Incense

Mix up a new incense to burn during your
incantations. Coltsfoot and lavender will inspire
love in all those lucky enough to cross your
path. Wormwood will protect you from any meddle-
some wandering spirits along the way. Using the
back of a spoon, crush together 1 tablespoon each
dried coltsfoot, lavender, and wormwood.
Stir in 1 tablespoon cornstarch.

Or try this irresistible love-inducing voodoo mixture:
Crush together 1 tablespoon each dried dill, marjoram,
and cornstarch. Stir in 3 drops vanilla extract.

Sprinkle 1 teaspoon of your mixture of choice
on the center of a lighted incense coal during
your charm creation.

Love Me Philter

Create a love-inspiring anointing oil in one of your
vials. Basil encourages love and even has its own
Hindu goddess, Tulsi. Cardamom has long been recog-
nized as a potent ardor-inducing medicine, causing the
unsuspecting to fall violently in love. Mix together
a few drops of each of these essential oils: basil,
cardamom, and anise. Sprinkle a few drops of the
anointing oil on your charms as you make them.

Lover's Lane

Collect a handful of white stones, or pull the
petals from a white flower. Walk from your love's
home to yours; occasionally drop a pebble or petal
as you go. Now love will know the way.

Gypsy Name Game

★ ★ ★

If you have too many potential honeys from which
to choose, try this Gypsy name divination. Cut out
a star from a sheet of paper, giving it as many rays
as you have sweethearts' names. Write one name
on each ray, beginning the name at the center of
the star and finishing it at the point of the ray.
Find an acorn and tie a red silk thread to its cap.
Acorns are lucky and come from the strong and
faithful oak. They mean business! Dangle the nut over
the center of the star. Slowly it will begin to swing
along one of the names. Bingo! We have a winner.

Bewitching Basics

o o o o

CONCOCTING MAGIC IS MORE THAN JUST TOSSING AN EYE OF
NEWT INTO A BOILING CAULDRON. YOU MUST CONCENTRATE
ALL YOUR ENERGY, DREAMS, AND DESIRES INTO EACH CHARM.
CLEAR YOUR MIND COMPLETELY OF ALL RANDOM THOUGHTS
AND CONCENTRATE ON YOUR OBJECTIVE WHILE MIXING UP
YOUR POTIONS AND CHANTING YOUR INCANTATIONS.
THINKING ABOUT THE BOY OF YOUR DREAMS, THOSE CUTE
SHOES YOU SAW ON YOUR WAY HOME, *AND* THE PLANTS THAT
NEED WATERING IS LIKELY TO CAUSE A TERRIBLE WITCHY
IMPLOSION. YOU COULD END UP WITH A BOYFRIEND WHO
SITS ON THE COUCH LIKE A POTTED PLANT. IT WILL BE POOR
CONSOLATION INDEED THAT HE WEARS CUTE SHOES.

We all know about these! They are known as poppets in Celtic magic. The sooner you make one, the sooner things will start going your way. Every girl needs a zombie love slave to follow her every command. If your sweetie doesn't behave, give the doll a good poke with a pin. And then kiss your love to make it better.

Voodoo Dolls

Gingerbread man cookie cutter, about 4 by 6 inches

Cotton fabric in a color or pattern that reminds you of your love, 8 by 10 inches

Pencil

Scissors

Needle and thread

Choose a mixture of these dried herbs and plants: meadowsweet, wheat, mint, catnip, comfrey, marjoram, myrtle, and rue

Beads and sequins

A photo of "the One" (optional)

A personal item from your honey

Using the cookie cutter for a template, trace its outline onto one half of the fabric with the pencil. Cut out around the outline with the scissors. Repeat with the remaining half. Stack the cutouts, right sides facing inwards. Using the needle and thread, sew the cutouts together along the edge, leaving a 1-inch opening.

Turn the fabric right-side out and stuff it with the herbal mixture. Decorate the doll with bead and sequin facial features. If you happen to have a photo of "the One," sew this in place instead.

Now you will need a personal item. Something really personal is best, such as a lock or strand of hair or a scrap or thread of clothing. The more you have the better. Obviously it might be a bit awkward to snip a chunk of his hair surreptitiously. And, if caught, you would definitely come off as a raving lunatic who should be avoided! As an alternative, just get something he's touched. "Can I borrow your pen?" Then pocket it! Sew the personal item(s) inside the doll or, if more appropriate, to the outside.

Place the doll on your altar to direct your thoughts and focus your energy during charm making.

ᴄ Love Lore ᴄ

ON A WEDNESDAY, BLOW DRIED RUE TOWARD
YOUR LOVER'S HOME AND THE OBJECT OF YOUR
AFFECTION WILL SHOW UP.

You Flirt! Bath

Flirty daisies worn on a midsummer's eve bring the blessings of the fairies. Celtic maidens wove daisy chains in their hair to attract a beloved's attention. Stick a daisy behind your ear before you head out and about to add a kick to your step.

This bath will heighten your flirting powers while making your skin as happy as your heart. Draw a hot tub; fill it with fresh daisy petals, 1/2 cup dried lavender, 2 tablespoons ground cinnamon, and 1/2 cup nonfat milk powder; and slip into it for a nice, long soak.

Binding Love to You

Be forewarned that forcing someone to do something against his or her will is a serious decision, and a binding spell can do just that. Remember, too, you're not just binding him; you're also binding yourself. You had better be sure you want to be bound to this guy—forever! Use with caution.

Make a poppet doll of yourself using the instructions for Voodoo Dolls (page 54). Bind your doll and his together with a red ribbon for passion, a pink ribbon for romance, and an orange ribbon for friendship. Tie each ribbon around and around the poppets in 7 knots. Following the voodoo tradition, place the dolls under your bed. Or try the European custom of burying them at a crossroads.

Gypsy Magic Pouch

Cut out a 6-inch square of fabric. Place 1 tablespoon
dried rue in the center. Top with something
personal from the one you love. Gather up the corners
of the square and tie together with a red ribbon.
Hang the pouch on your bedpost on the new moon,
and leave it there until the full moon. By then
he will have contacted you.

Love Lore

GYPSIES USE WONDERFUL AND WHIMSICAL LOVE TALISMANS:
APPLES, ACORNS, BELLS, KEYS, BIRD'S EGGS, AND PEAS
IN A POD. ADD ANY AND ALL TO THE GYPSY MAGIC POUCH
FOR EXTRA ZING.

Cracking a Stony Heart

Over the course of 7 days, find 13 small pebbles. Look for ones that immediately attract your attention. On the first Friday of the waxing moon, go to a grassy spot and arrange the stones in a little heart shape. Lie down on the stones with your heart on the stone heart. Think of your love. Then arrange the stones into your love's initials. Lie down on the stone initials and think of yourself. This will bring you to your love's mind. Pick up the stones and carry them with you until the full moon. If it is meant to be, it will be.

 Herbs & Flowers

OOH LA LA!—FRENCH PERFUME MAKERS KNOW WHICH *MAGIQUE* SCENTS MAKE THE HEART FLIP. THE STRONGEST HEART SCENTS ARE CLARY SAGE, VERBENA, CLOVE, AND CINNAMON. USE ANY OR ALL TO ATTRACT YOUR LOVER'S ATTENTION. *TRÈS MAGNIFIQUE!*

Key to His Heart

Voodoo charms can be a little spooky. That's what
makes them fun! Find an old key (you should not
know what it unlocks). Light a black candle and a
white candle and burn It's You Baby Incense (page 50).
Face toward your lover's direction. Through the hole
in the top of the key, inhale as you whisper your
lover's name. Press the key into warm, softened
beeswax. Mold the wax around the key into the shape
of a person. Let the wax cool. Tie a white ribbon
around the wax-encased key, tying with 9 knots.
Carry the talisman with you.

Enchanted Doorway

Find a doorway through which your lover is
sure to pass. Sprinkle dried rosemary along the
threshold that will go unnoticed by anyone passing
over it. While you sprinkle, repeat your honey's
name and yours 3 times. Walk away without
stepping through the doorway or looking back.
The next unattached person to cross the threshold
will be yours. Let's hope it's the right one! Enchanting
your doorway and inviting your honey over can
help prevent unwanted suitors.

∽ Love Lore ∾

ERZULIE IS THE VOODOO GODDESS OF LOVE. AFRICAN SLAVES
BROUGHT THEIR TRIBAL BELIEFS TO HAITI IN THE SIXTEENTH
CENTURY, WHERE THEY COMBINED WITH LOCAL TRADITIONS
AND EVENTUALLY SPREAD TO LOUISIANA AND ELSEWHERE IN
THE SOUTH. ERZULIE IS ADMIRED AND FEARED BECAUSE SHE
REPRESENTS LOVE BUT ALSO JEALOUSY. SHE DEMANDS THE
MOST FROM HER FOLLOWERS, PREFERRING AN ENTIRE ROOM
DEVOTED TO HER WORSHIP. SHE LIKES KISSING, DANCING, AND
SPEAKING FRENCH. WOO HER WITH SUGARY DRINKS.

Too busy for the home version? A pocket-size altar for the girl-on-the-go gives you everything you need to perform a ritual anywhere and everywhere.

Go-Go Girl Matchbox Altar

Glue

2 color copies of a love deity, about 1½ by 2 inches

Small matchbox

Glitter and rhinestones

Scissors

Red cloth

Love herb that works for you, such as dried rue

Pink embroidery thread

Rose quartz stone

1 birthday candle

1 match

Love Me Philter (page 51)

Glue a color copy of a love deity to the bottom interior and to the exterior top of the matchbox sleeve. Embellish the top by gluing on glitter and rhinestones. Using the scissors, trim the red cloth into a 1-inch square. Sprinkle a small amount of a love herb on the center of the cloth. Gather up the corners of the square and tie together with the embroidery thread. Place the pouch inside the box. Add the stone, the birthday candle, and the match to the box. Anoint the inside with a drop of Love Me Philter. Slide on the box top and you're off!

Fire, Water, and Voodoo! Oh My!

In a glass bowl that has never been used, mix together
1/2 cup of water gathered from a flowing spring,
dash of Tabasco sauce, 1 tablespoon fresh or dried
rosemary, 5 drops Love Me Philter (page 51), and
1 drop red wine. Stir clockwise with your finger.
Sprinkle this mixture around the house of your secret
love on 3 consecutive nights during the full moon.
Now he is yours.

✧ Love Lore ✧

MANY ANCIENT IRISH LOVE CHARMS WERE WRITTEN
IN BLOOD WITH A RAVEN'S QUILL. FOR THE FAINT
OF HEART, RED WINE IS A PERFECT SUBSTITUTE.

Genie in a Bottle Charm

☆ ☆ ☆

Fill one of your clear glass vials with a photo of
your love, a handful of jewels, a few crystals, and
glitter. Real jewels work best, but plastic are okay.
Add a pinch of dried marigold petals and a pinch
of ground cardamom. Fill the vial with springwater
and a drop of blue food coloring and cap it.

Shake up the vial and place it in a sunny
window to charge. After 7 days, open the top to
release the genie magic. Give him a few moments
(he needs time to stretch after all), then politely
order him to do your bidding.

Oh-So-Sweetheart

Find a small, clear plastic container. A gum-machine orb is perfect. Fill it up with a few chocolate kisses for love, Hot Tamales for passion, Sweet Tarts for the yin-yang thing, Root Beer Barrels to keep things funky, and Laffy Taffy for laughs, of course. Recite this incantation while you add the candies:

You are so sweet, you're good enough to eat.

When you are mine, I will be thine.

Toss the candies-loaded container to your honey and walk away.

Bewitching Basics

○ ○ ○ ○

INCANTATION WRITING 101—ROMANIAN LOVE CHARMS ARE
ALMOST ENTIRELY SPOKEN INCANTATIONS, SONGS OR CHANTS
PASSED THROUGH THE GENERATIONS BY WORD OF MOUTH.
MANY CELTIC INCANTATIONS, CHILDHOOD RHYMES WE ALL
KNOW, HAVE ALSO STOOD THE TEST OF TIME AND ARE ALWAYS
USEFUL. BUT WRITING YOUR OWN INCANTATIONS ALLOWS YOU
TO TAILOR THE CHARM TO YOUR SPECIFIC DESIRES.

INCANTATIONS USUALLY RHYME. THIS MAKES THEM CATCHY
AND EASY TO REMEMBER, BUT ALSO GIVES THEM A RHYTHM FOR
CHANTING, AIDING YOUR CONCENTRATION AND MEDITATION.
IF YOU'RE A DUNCE AT POETRY, PLOP YOURSELF DOWN WITH A
RHYMING DICTIONARY FOR ASSISTANCE. ASSEMBLE A LIST OF
WORDS THAT RHYME WITH YOUR NAME, WITH YOUR BELOVED'S
NAME, AND WITH OTHER SIMPLE WORDS SUCH AS *ME, MINE,*
AND *LOVE*. THEN CONSTRUCT SHORT PHRASES WITH AN EQUAL
NUMBER OF SYLLABLES, AND END EACH LINE WITH ONE OF THE
RHYMING WORDS. COUPLETS ARE THE EASIEST WAY TO BEGIN.
RELAX, IT'S FUN! IF ALL ELSE FAILS, CHOOSE A FAVORITE SONG
AND CHANGE THE WORDS TO SUIT YOUR PURPOSE.

INCANTATIONS NEED TO BE POSITIVE AND POWERFUL. FOR
INSTANCE, USE THE WORD "WILL" *NOT* "WISH" OR "HOPE."
NO SCAREDY-CAT HEXES HERE.

Apples, which bring good luck and inspire love, have been the bearers of charms and curses since the first fateful bite. It seems that nobody can resist their sweet juiciness, nor escape their natural heart shape.

Apple of My Eye

Enchanted Apple Charm

Pick a half green–half red apple during the full moon. Polish it with a scarf you have worn. Breathe on the red side while thinking of your true love and whispering the following:

Passion red
And true love green
Ignite the heart
And turn the head.

Now, eat the green half, and then kiss the red half and place it in your lover-to-be's hand. He who holds it will fall in love. He who eats it will be yours.

Fifteenth-Century Celtic Apple Charm

Carve the words "Guel & Bsatirell & Gliaell" into an apple. Give it to your heart's desire to eat, and he will be yours.

Three Gypsy Apple Divination Charms

Apple Charm No. 1: Get an apple from a widow without thanking her. This may sound difficult, but it just means you need to know more about your grocery clerk than you may now. Eat one half before the stroke of midnight and the other half after midnight. You will dream of your future love. This charm works best during the full moon.

continued

Apple Charm No. 2: Peel an apple in an unbroken spiral. (This is a magic trick in itself!) Toss the peel on the ground. It will form the first initial of your future true love.

Apple Charm No. 3: Twist an apple stem clockwise while reciting the letters of the alphabet. When the stem breaks, the letter you have just said is the first initial of your future love. (What will become of all the Zacks in the world?)

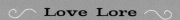

∽ Love Lore ∾

THERE ARE NINETY-SIX WORDS FOR LOVE IN SANSKRIT,
EIGHTY IN ANCIENT PERSIAN, THREE IN GREEK, AND ONE
IN ENGLISH. NOT VERY ROMANTIC, BUT, HEY, IT MAKES
INCANTATION WRITING A SNAP!

Tarot Ties

Shuffle through a tarot card deck and find the Star
(you), the Knight of Cups (him), and the Lovers
(the two of you together). Line these up in the middle
of your altar table with the card of the lovers
in the center. Place a small glass of springwater
on top of your card, another small glass of springwater
on top of his, and an empty glass on the card
of the lovers. Light 13 red candles. Simultaneously
pour the water from the full glasses into the empty
glass while visualizing the joining of your
two hearts as one.

Airmail Valentine Charm

At your altar, write a letter to your love, including in it all the reasons you love him so. Anoint each corner of the stationery with Love Me Philter (page 51). Using your finger, trace the 4 points together in a clockwise circle. Sprinkle the center with a pinch of fresh, love-inspiring lemon verbena. Fold the paper into an airplane, and then continue to fold with the herb in the center, visualizing your goal being enacted and fulfilled as you work and making the paper as small as possible. Wind pink thread around and around the paper while repeating your desired's name. Tie the thread with 3 knots and address the outside of the letter. Keep the message in your pocket until such time as you feel comfortable delivering it.

∾ Love Lore ∾

MARGERY BREWS OF ENGLAND SENT THE
FIRST VALENTINE IN 1477.

This magical and modern oracle looks like a swirling galaxy. A chip of beryl stone encourages visions and assists with love divination.

Magic 8 Ball Oracle

Polymer clay

Toothpick

Small, clear jar with a tight fitting top (such as a baby-food jar)

Light corn syrup

Glitter and metallic confetti in celestial shapes

Chip of polished beryl

Form the polymer clay into a triangular or square three-dimensional shape, no larger than about 1 inch square. Using the toothpick, inscribe each side with an answer, such as "yes," "no," "perhaps," or something more mystical.

Bake the polymer shape in the oven according to the package directions. When it has cooled, place it in the bottom of the jar. Fill the jar to two-thirds full with corn syrup. Sprinkle in the glitter and metallic confetti, and the beryl. Top up the jar with water, and screw on the cap *very* tightly.

Shake the jar and think of a question. Turn the jar right-side up and the magic oracle will float down and let you read the answer through the bottom.

Chapter 3

Beguile–Head-over-Heels in Love

Suddenly, you find yourself acting all wrong. Why are you buying expensive, frilly underthings that clash with your witchy wardrobe? That's easy, it's love! Now that you've found "the One," the fun really begins.

When you're able to tear yourself away from staring into your sweetheart's starry eyes, flip through this chapter for delectable elixirs to share, delicious charms to devour, and the sweetest tokens of affection to give your love.

Red-hot red is the color of the day. Spread your altar with a red scarf and gather red candles, red flowers, and a few of these hot-to-trot items: hibiscus, ginger, passionflower, papaya, cinnamon, cardamom, and jasmine.

Instant Attraction Incense

Mix up this potent incense while falling in love. Galangal and basil are love-inspiring herbs used in East Indian charms. A touch of allspice fuels the fire. Using the back of a spoon, crush together 1 tablespoon each dried galangal, basil, and allspice. Stir 1 tablespoon cornstarch into the mixture. Add 1 drop cinnamon oil for extra kick. Sprinkle 1 teaspoon of the mixture on the center of a lighted incense coal to burn while you are making charms and whenever your honey is near.

First Love Philter

Buckle your seat belt! These three spicy oils ignite the inner spitfire. In a vial, combine 10 drops clove oil, 5 drops ginger oil, and 5 drops peppermint oil. Anoint your candles, your charms—and your wrists if you dare.

Herbs & Flowers

SCENT AN ENTIRE ROOM WITH YOUR LOVE PHILTERS WITHOUT LIGHTING A MATCH. MODERN TIMES CALL FOR MODERN METHODS. DAB ONE OF YOUR LOVE PHILTERS ON A LOW-WATT LIGHTBULB, AND THE WARM BULB WILL DIFFUSE THE SCENT THROUGHOUT THE ROOM, SENDING ROMANCE INTO EVERY NOOK AND CRANNY.

Pucker up! Lip-soothing balms are imbued with essential oils sure to inspire blind devotion in anyone lucky enough to be kissed. Kissable vanilla will imprint your lips in his memory; it revs up love and lust, but is also one of the most memorable scents. Yummy cherry adds a rosy gleam while inciting lust. Strawberries nourish love, especially when the berries are shared.

Kissing Balm

½ teaspoon beeswax

1 teaspoon coconut oil

Small microwave-safe bowl

Wooden spoon

1 tablespoon almond oil

4 drops vanilla oil

Scissors

1 vitamin E capsule

A few drops cherry or strawberry flavoring oil

Place the beeswax and coconut oil in the bowl and microwave on high until melted, about 1 minute. Do not overheat. Using the wooden spoon, stir in the almond and vanilla oils. Using the scissors, snip the end off the vitamin E capsule and squeeze the oil into the mixture. If you like, add flavor by stirring in a few drops of cherry or strawberry oil. Pour the mixture into an empty lip balm or cosmetics container. Let cool.

If you'd prefer to use the classic cauldron method, heat the beeswax and coconut oil on the stove top in a double boiler. Remove from heat and proceed as directed.

Candy Kisses

Chocolate charms are wasted on those who don't appreciate their wicked wiles. Save this treat for a chocolate lover who likes to share. Customize a bag of chocolate kisses so that your honey knows just what you have in mind.

Carefully unwrap the candies. Remove the inner white strip of tissue paper and trace the outline onto pink writing paper. Trim out as many strips from the pink paper as you will need. Using a red pen, write one reason you love your sweetie on each slip of paper. If you can't think of at least fifty, easy, it's time to return to chapter 1! Wrap a message around each kiss. Then rewrap the foil around the candies so that a pink paper note peeks out the top of each one. Place the kisses in a box that you have decorated with tons of glitter and plastic jewels.

Only you topped with frosting would be a sweeter dessert! The orange yumminess of these ruby red cupcakes will make your love forget their potent falling-in-love powers. Blood orange seals romantic love, vanilla inspires love, and roses are the flowers of Venus. Legend has it that Venus pricked her finger on the thorn of a white rose, releasing a drop of her blood that stained the rose red. Since then red roses have been associated with romance, making them one of the most common ingredients in love charms.

Lovely Cupcakes

1 box white cake mix

Milk

Unsalted butter

2 teaspoons vanilla extract

6 drops blood orange oil

3 dried red rose petals, crushed

Red food coloring

2 muffin pans lined with paper liners (12 cupcakes total)

1 container pink frosting

Candy toppings: all your favorites—such as Red Hots, gummy hearts, and red sprinkles—and maybe a few of his, too

Whip up the cake mix according to the package directions. Yummify the mix by using milk for the box recipe's liquid ingredient (usually water) and real butter instead of shortening or oil. This will make any mix taste homemade. Stir the mixture clockwise and envision the binding of your love.

Add the vanilla extract, blood orange oil, rose petals, and enough red food coloring to make the batter racy red. Mix thoroughly. Pour the batter into the prepared muffin pans.

Bake according to the package directions. Remove from the oven and let cool. Frost each cupcake with the pink frosting, and decorate with lots of red candies and sprinkles. Share a cupcake with your honey tonight, for the absolutely quickest way to his heart.